My more-than-coloring book about

ME

Cathy Spieler

Illustrated by Ed Koehler

Cover illustrations by Alex Zisser,

with help from Adam Singer, Melanie Johnson,

Hannah Miles, and Bradley Vogelsmeier

CPH®
SAINT LOUIS

Thank you to the children at Christ Community Lutheran School in St. Louis, MO, who worked hard to give us pictures to choose from for the cover of this book. Each picture was delightful and creative!

All Scripture quotations, unless otherwise indicated, are taken from the HOLY BIBLE, NEW INTERNATIONAL VERSION®. NIV®. Copyright © 1973, 1978, 1984 by International Bible Society. Used by permission of Zondervan Publishing House. All rights reserved.

Copyright © 1999 Concordia Publishing House
3558 S. Jefferson Avenue, St. Louis, MO 63118-3968
Manufactured in the United States of America

Teachers who purchase this product may reproduce pages for classroom use. Parents and other individuals who purchase this product may reproduce pages as needed for in-home completion of activities.

All rights reserved. Except as noted above, no part of this publication may be reproduced, stored in a retrieval system, or transmitted, in any form or by any means, electronic, mechanical, photocopying, recording, or otherwise, without the prior written permission of Concordia Publishing House.

1   2   3   4   5   6   7   8   9   10   08   07   06   05   04   03   02   01   00   99

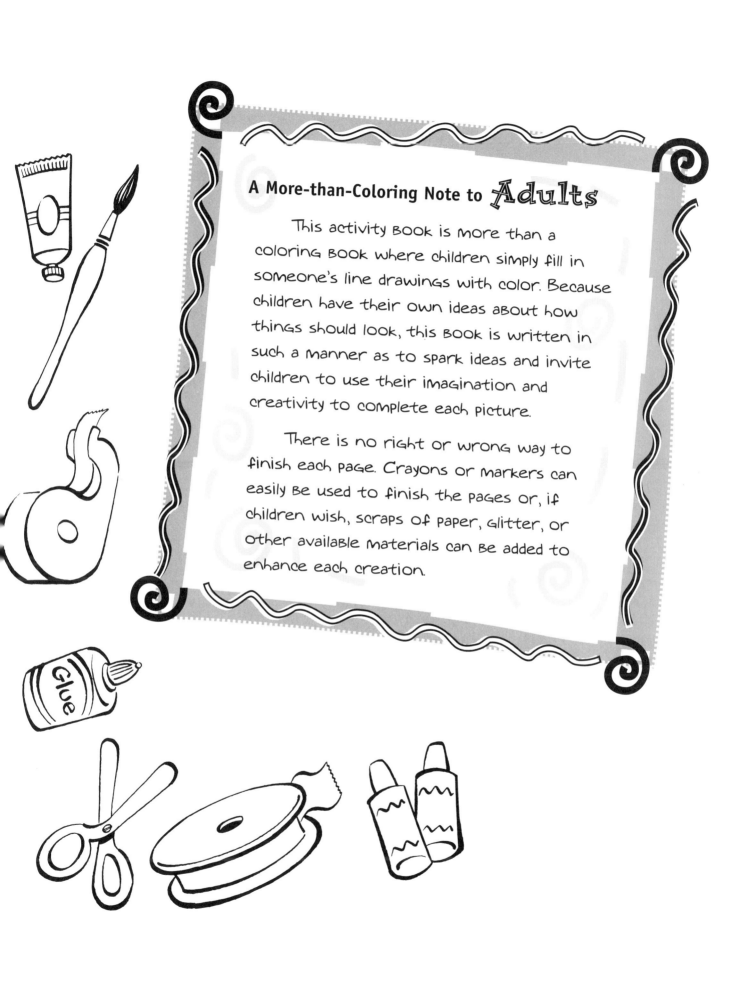

A More-than-Coloring Note to *Adults*

This activity book is more than a coloring book where children simply fill in someone's line drawings with color. Because children have their own ideas about how things should look, this book is written in such a manner as to spark ideas and invite children to use their imagination and creativity to complete each picture.

There is no right or wrong way to finish each page. Crayons or markers can easily be used to finish the pages or, if children wish, scraps of paper, glitter, or other available materials can be added to enhance each creation.

A More-than-Coloring Note for Children

The pages in this book are not finished. They are waiting for your great ideas and artistic creativity to make them complete.

Have someone read the words on each page to you or read them yourself. Then think about your ideas and decide how you would finish the picture.

God has given you great gifts and abilities. It's your turn to use them to make your own more-than-coloring masterpiece!

Draw a picture of yourself in this frame. Then color the frame. You are very special to God. There is no one just like you.

So God created man in His own image, in the image of God He created him. (Genesis 1:27)

5

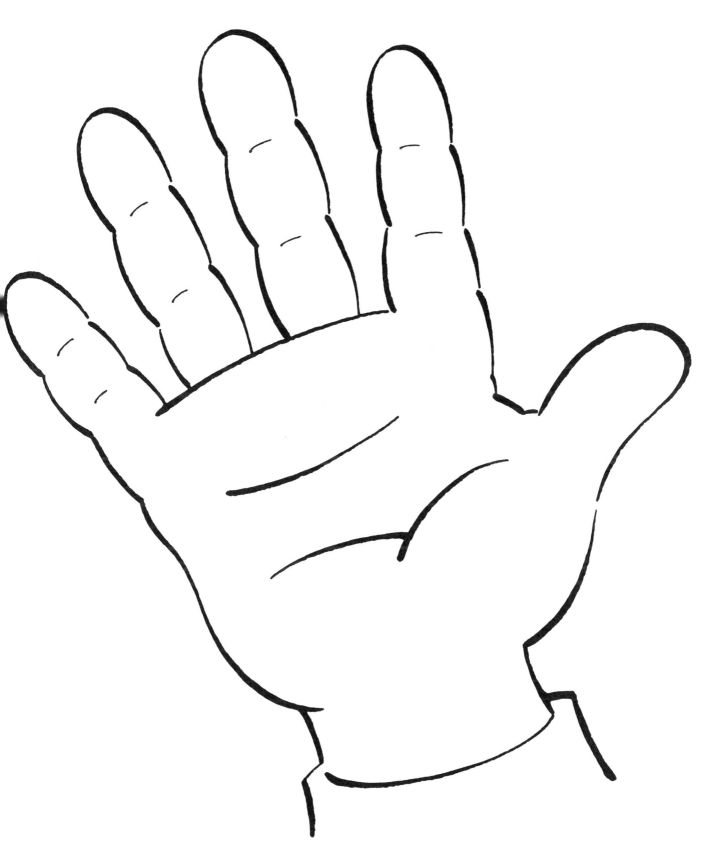

Your fingerprints are unique. No one else has fingerprints like yours. Use an ink pad, or scribble with a pencil and rub your finger over the pencil marks. Press your fingerprints onto the fingers of this hand.

Then God said, "Let Us make man in Our image, in Our likeness." (Genesis 1:26)

This is where I Live.

Draw the place that you call home on this page.

But He blesses the home of the righteous. (Proverbs 3:33)

Pretend this is your room. Draw your bed, dresser, and any other furniture you have in your room at home.

In My Father's house are many rooms …
I am going there to prepare a place for you. (John 14:2)

What would a book about you look like? Design the cover and make up a title so this book can be all about you.

Whatever you do, work at it with all your heart, as working for the Lord. (Colossians 3:23)

Did you ever wonder what you would look like with different hair?
Draw different kinds of hair on each of these faces.
Which one do you like best?

Indeed, the very hairs of your head are all numbered. (Luke 12:7)

Draw your favorite kind of cereal.
Or make up a new kind.
Don't forget to design the cover of the cereal box.

He has filled the hungry with good things. (Luke 1:53)

What does your best friend look like?
Finish drawing him or her on this page.
God gives us friends to help us.

A friend loves at all times. (Proverbs 17:17)

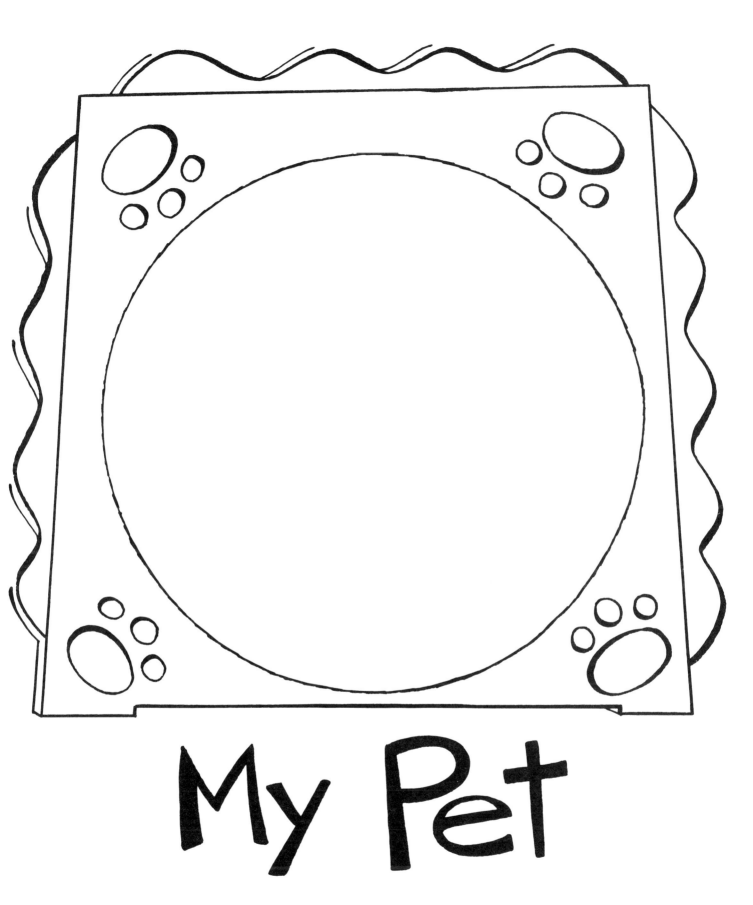

My Pet

Draw a picture of your pet here. If you don't have a pet, draw a picture of the pet you would like to have.

God made…all the creatures that move along the ground. (Genesis 1:25)

21

We all seem to have a favorite shirt that we like to wear a lot. Draw your favorite shirt.

For He has clothed me with garments of salvation and arrayed me in a robe of righteousness. (Isaiah 61:10)

God has placed you in a family that loves you.
Draw your family in the picture frame.

"Go home to your family and tell them how much the Lord has done for you, and how He has had mercy on you." (Mark 5:19)

God is with us as we go to school or on vacation.
Pretend your family is going on a trip. Draw them in the car.

[Jesus said,] "I am with you always." (Matthew 28:20)

What kind of birthday cake did you have for your last birthday?
How many candles were on it?
Decorate this birthday cake and place candles on it.

But grow in the grace and knowledge of our Lord and Savior Jesus Christ.
(2 Peter 3:18)

God has given us food to nourish our bodies.
Draw your favorite foods on this plate.

Give thanks to the LORD, for He is good. (Psalm 107:1)

If you were going on a trip, what would you take?
Fill this suitcase with things you might need.

Whoever trusts in the LORD is kept safe. (Proverbs 29:25)

Pretend you have packed for your trip.
How will you get to where you are going?
Draw the way you would like to travel on this page.

Blessed is the man who trusts in the LORD. (Jeremiah 17:7)

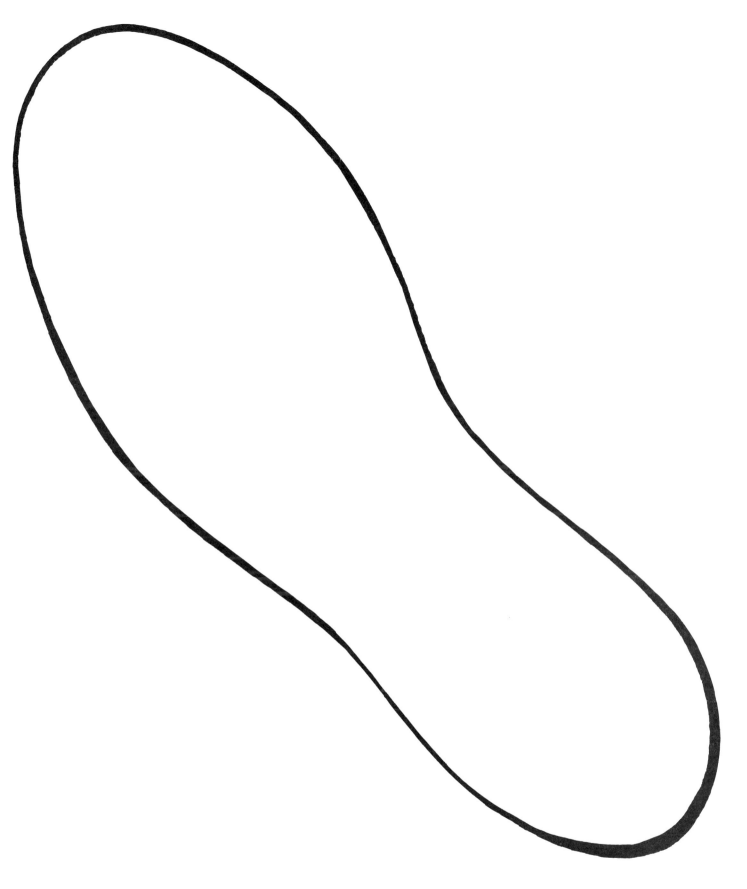

𝕯𝖔𝖊𝖘 your foot fit here?
Trace your foot inside the footprint.
Or look at the bottom of your shoe and draw the same design here.

Your Word is a lamp to my feet and a light for my path. (Psalm 119:105)

Do you like ice cream? What flavor would you choose? Draw your favorite flavor on this cone. Will you draw one scoop or two?

Taste and see that the LORD is good. (Psalm 34:8a)

Do you go to school?
What does your school look like? Draw it on this page.
Remember that God goes with you to school.

The LORD is near to all who call on Him. (Psalm 145:18)

What does your teacher look like?
Draw a picture of your teacher here.

It was He who gave some to be … teachers. (Ephesians 4:11)

What is your favorite thing to do when you play?
Draw a picture of your favorite activity here.

Put [your] hope in God, who richly provides us with everything for our enjoyment.
(1 Timothy 6:17)

God created things in beautiful colors.
What is your favorite color?
Finish this picture using your favorite colors.

He has made everything beautiful in its time. (Ecclesiastes 3:11)

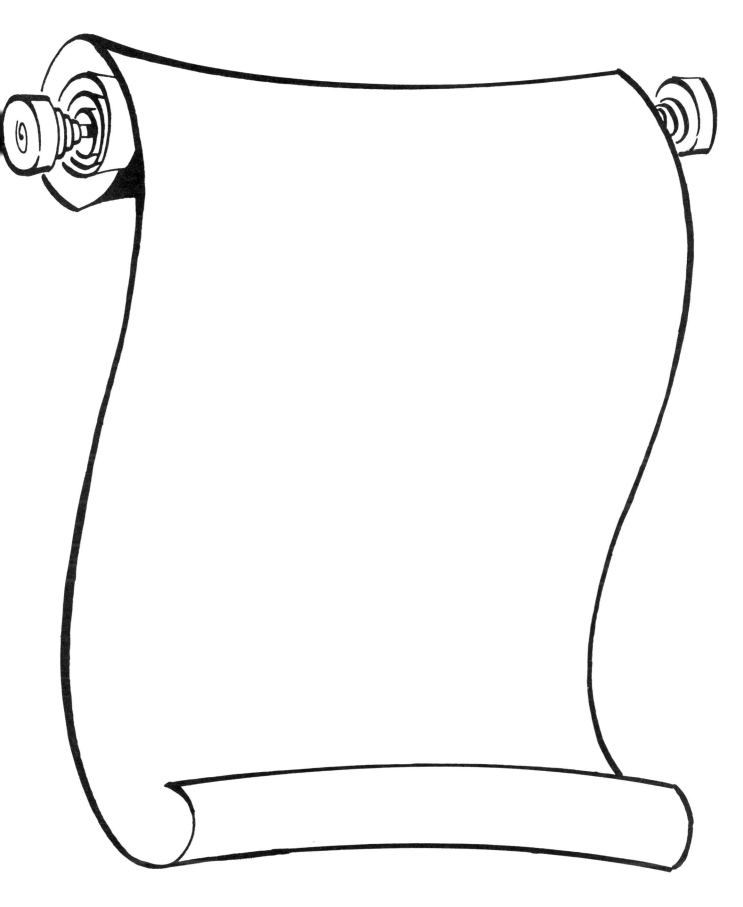

Do you have a favorite Bible story?
Draw a picture of the story on this scroll.

But the plans of the LORD stand firm forever. (Psalm 33:11)

God gives us friends. Draw a picture of your friends.
Remember that Jesus is your forever Friend.

[Jesus said,] "…I have called you friends…" (John 15:15)

If you could wish for something, what would it be?
Draw a picture of your wish on this page.

Search me, O God, and know my heart. (Psalm 140:23a)

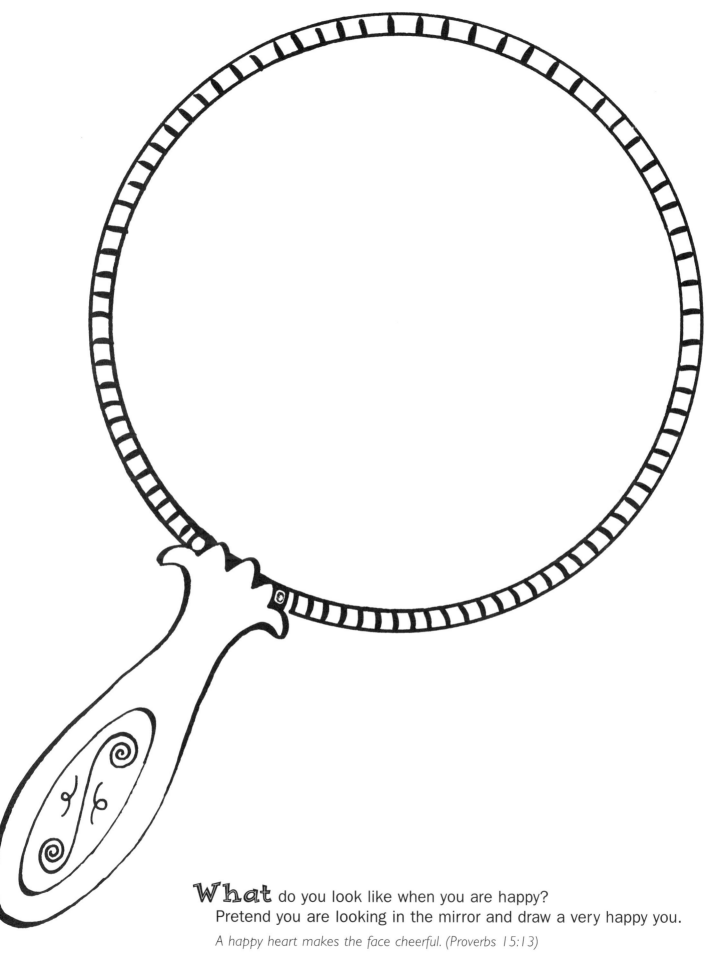

What do you look like when you are happy?
Pretend you are looking in the mirror and draw a very happy you.

A happy heart makes the face cheerful. (Proverbs 15:13)

It's fun to get gifts.
Draw something you would like to receive as a gift.

Every good and perfect gift is from above,
coming down from the Father of the heavenly lights. (James 1:17)

If you could be in the circus, what would you be?
Draw yourself as a circus star.

Many, O Lord my God, are the wonders You have done. (Psalm 40:5)

Did you ever want to build a tree house and play in a tree like a bird? Draw a tree house in this tree.

Surely goodness and love will follow me all the days of my life,
and I will dwell in the house of the LORD forever. (Psalm 23:6)

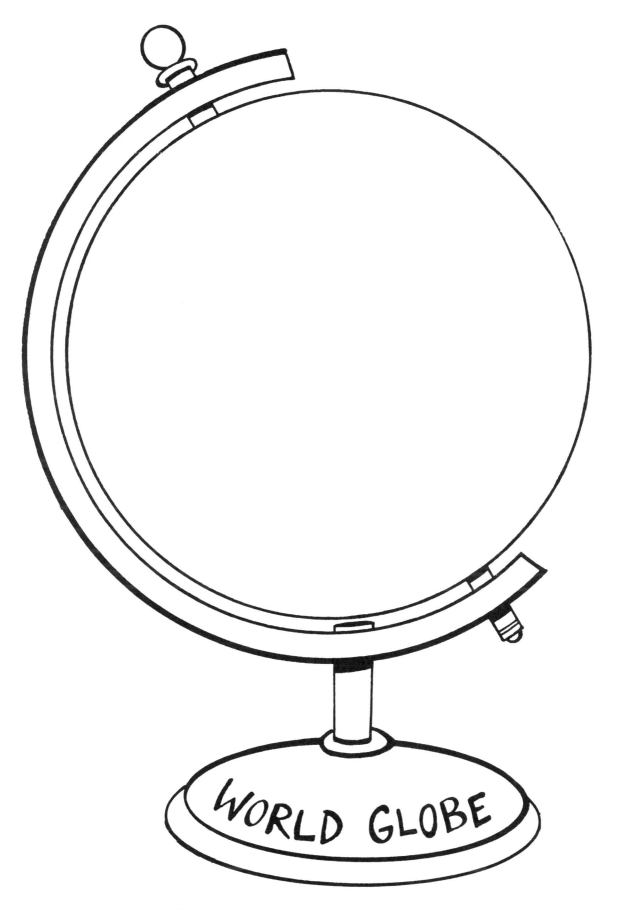

You are a child of God, part of God's family.
Draw a picture of you with others in the family of God.

You … have been taught by God to love each other. (1 Thessalonians 4:9)

The End